SIMPLE
METHODS
SMARTER
DECISIONS

Safety Resources for

Female Recording Artists

Author

LATOYA COOPER

The Songstress

Music Meets The Boardroom, LLC
1169 N Burleson Blvd.
#350
Burleson, Texas 76028

www.MusicMeetsTheBoardroom.com
Ordering Information:
For Details Email Contact@MusicMeetsTheBoardroom.com

Print ISBN: 978-0-578-96757-8
eBook ISBN: 978-1-63848-644-2
Printed in the United States of America on SFI Certified Paper.
First Edition

HEY SUPERSTAR!

Are you thinking about or preparing to release a music single? There are important steps to take in your business before releasing music to the world.

Here is a freebie to support your progress!

Download the "25 Steps To Take Before Releasing Your Music Single" Checklist NOW!

* It's FREE, Plus 5 Bonus Steps Are Included!

https://www.musicmeetstheboardroom.com/freebies-pbook

TABLE OF CONTENTS

INTRODUCTION

I felt compelled to write this book after noticing an underlying pattern within the music industry on many levels. It is an issue that has been going on for years, but unfortunately, as women, we have a hard time getting ahead of it.

2019, 2020 and 2021 served as powerful years of truth—especially for the music and entertainment community. Women of all ages and backgrounds felt compelled to come forward sharing life-changing stories in numbers we have not seen in past years. Some of these stories include bringing illegal activities surrounding the mistreatment of women by powerful people in the music industry, and unfavorable business practices that impact legacy to light. However, the most alarming aspect to these stories, and likely why they garnered national attention, is that they involved many well-connected executives and mega superstars.

As I finish the final details of this book, even more influential men and women in the music industry are being called out or charged with allegations involving the physical or sexual abuse of women and young girls. There are also stories coming to light surrounding the theft of brands and intellectual property created by various musical artists. Many of these cases are still pending in the courts and continue to dominate the headlines. The stories have been disturbing and the details at times are unimaginable to digest.

It is interesting how the world is so wrapped up in these cases; powerful people using their platforms to use and abuse others is nothing new.

However, the news coverage brought something else to mind for me; all I can think about is all the other women in the music industry who did not have a voice or platform to share their stories.

INTRODUCTION

It made me think about my personal stories and experiences as a young recording artist eager for opportunity. Due to my trusting spirit and lack of experience, I was an easy target. When I think about my personal journey, as well as the stories that have been shared with me, I know my counterparts and I will neither be the first nor the last. When will we see it end?

I am emotional as I write this, triggered by the news stories. I can only imagine the numerous women who have been exposed to unhealthy environments throughout their musical journey. Individuals who do not care about women's best interests come from all races, economic backgrounds, sex and environments.

It is interesting how taboo this topic is. As a community, we do not often talk about this subject nor provide any help, tips or recommendations for female artists entering into the music industry. Some of the advice is so simple; it could help so many and even save a life. Yet, collectively as a music community of women, we do not take the time to reinforce the knowledge—why is that? Is it due to shame or fear? Has this become the norm in society, or has it always been? Have we become desensitized to this kind of behavior? Well, I certainly have not!

We cannot control nor should we carry the responsibility for the actions of others. However, we can empower each other to better understand the game we are in and maneuver these streets with as much shared knowledge as possible. It starts by sharing, sharing, sharing... information is power!

Share your story with as many female artists who will listen. Do not wait until after a negative experience; share the lessons you have learned throughout your journey.

It is important to remind fellow women of their self-worth and value. Remind them that they are worthy of being protected and that it is okay to establish and maintain boundaries without guilt.

It is important women feel confident with having a voice and are comfortable standing up for themselves. As a woman, you need to understand that you have a right to safety and protection. Most importantly, you need to know you are WORTH protecting. You deserve to feel safe as you work in the creative community. This is not up for debate and should never be jeopardized or compromised.

My goal for this book is to help women of all ages entering or currently in the music business. I want to help women avoid the common pitfalls and uncomfortable situations that often occur in this industry. This subject is one that is very dear to me, as I have personally experienced situations that were not safe and could not think clearly in the moment. If I had access to more information and knew then what I know now, I could have applied *simple methods* and would have made *smarter decisions.*

As the CEO of Music Meets The Boardroom, we host an annual Indie Artist Power Conference focusing on "Women In Music". Over the years as an active artist, I have noticed that the women who are making strides in music have special concerns and unique needs only other women can understand and relate to. An important lesson I have learned is that women have to make decisions that support their safety in the music industry. We need support and tips we can keep in the forefront of our mind as we move forward, so we can remain focused on our musical missions. Let this book only be the beginning; the women following your journey need you to reach back as well!

Thank you for investing in you. By purchasing this book, you have taken a powerful step forward.

At the end of each chapter; you will find an opportunity to write down your thoughts and plan to apply the insight shared throughout this book. The content of this book was designed to work for you along your musical journey. So take what you have learned and take action!

Protect Your Spirit,
Energy, And Trusted Gift...

What Is Good And What Is Bad Is
Attracted To Your Light!

THE POWER OF YOUR GIFT

Vision is a Spiritual Gift. The ability to create beautiful art, like music, comes from a place of endless possibility within the imagination. While certain aspects of creativity can be taught, the gift of vision (the ability to see full pictures or finished compositions in your head) is a special and innate gift. It is very important for artists (more importantly female artists), to understand this. When you understand the nature in which your gift was given, you are more likely to protect it and see the immense value in protecting it. When you truly understand that your talent and art is a God-Given Gift you have been TRUSTED with, you have a completely different relationship with it.

You may be wondering, how is this? First, you have to understand that your creative gift is a tool to inspire and heal your community and world. It is a gift designed to help encourage and support people and ultimately make the world a better place. Your gift is designed to help others see what is possible and inspire them to move forward in action with their own dreams and possibilities! **YOUR GIFT CAN MOVE PEOPLE INTO ACTION!**

Unfortunately, this gift also encourages people to come forth in the world who want to exploit and destroy it. Why? Because it is extremely powerful! Your gift has the ability to empower people and communities. Your gift has the power to create unity. It also has the power to control and influence, and some people know this. They also know that many extremely talented people do not know and understand the power of the gift they hold. This can be a dangerous combination.

When you fully understand the power that exists within your creative spiritual gifts, you are more likely to be mindful of your surroundings. As a result, you become more aware of your presence and how it can affect the direction of your gift, life and the lives of others.

Being mindful of your gift, however, is not enough; spiritual health and connection with God are very important. This is not about religion; it is deeper than religion. Your gifts are spiritual, and you cannot have the spiritual gift without the spiritual connection. Spirituality may mean different things to different people, but regardless of what you believe in, you need to understand how valuable this connection is.

Once you start to tap into your gift the way God and the universe intend for you. Better equipped, you will be able to recognize when negative forces come into your life. For example, your gift is directly linked to greatness, and there are people (energy) who want to interfere with your gift's full potential. This is called spiritual warfare; it is important to study this so you learn to identify when you encounter it.

Once you understand that this force is present, you are more likely to make decisions that keep your gift protected. In addition, you will start to be mindful of your environment, the company you keep, and how this force may show up.

Have you ever noticed, gifted people often have spiritual and emotional struggles? This is because gifted people are deep thinkers, emotionally sensitive, and tend to experience the present moment in great transparent detail. This is part of their supernatural gift, but it comes with some struggle—between the spiritual gift, the world, and spiritual relationship with God. Everyone who has a deep soulful creative gift experiences this in one form or another.

Write down your thoughts about your spiritual gift:

What do you know about your spiritual gift at this point in your musical career?

____

____

____

____

____

____

What will you pay closer attention to as you move forward in relation to your spiritual gift?

____

____

____

____

____

____

14

How do you plan to keep yourself spiritually balanced and connected?

____

____

____

____

____

____

What steps will you take to keep your trusted gift close and dear to you?

____

____

____

____

____

____

15

Personal Relationships

Shape Professional Success....

Do not Invest Your

Valuable Time With Anyone You

Would Not Want To Be!

NEVER A SHORTAGE OF OPPORTUNITY

To keep yourself and your gift protected, be mindful of the company you keep; because it will affect your success, well-being and safety. Check your environment; be aware of your surroundings, friends and family practices. You are the company you keep! It does not mean putting up a guard in every social situation; it just means setting and implementing healthy boundaries you feel confident sticking to.

There are some industry environments that are popular and appealing, but before you enter into those circles, determine whether or not those particular areas will give your talent the best outcome. Sometimes people enter into certain circles within the industry without thinking about the consequences that come along with their involvement.

Every diamond is not precious or true. Take time to pull back the layers and see past the polished finish and shine. It may fool others, but do not let it fool you. Regardless of how popular or trendy something is, see everyone and everything for who and what is. Make the best decisions for yourself and your future even if you have to walk alone for a period of time.

Remember, your talent is a trusted gift. Where and how you use it will not only affect your life but those who are looking up to you as well. Choose healthy environments to expand and share your gifts with the world. It does not guarantee your safety, but it helps to reduce unnecessary issues and headaches. If you are serious about your gift, you will not have time for anything outside your focus.

Not all opportunities are good. If an environment includes drugs, alcohol and irresponsible activities, your gift is not likely to be used in the best way. Get comfortable with walking away from what is not healthy for you. Rest assured, there will always be another opportunity. There is no shortage of opportunity; it may come packaged differently, but what is meant to be yours will be yours!

Let go of the trained scarcity mindset that commonly flows within the music community. It has no place in your life!

In this industry, it is essential to build relationships with high-achieving individuals with like-minded positive values. These people will be your new friends, associates and accountability partners.

While you may see some positive gains from wild social parties and gatherings fueled by industry politics and popularity pressure, see it for what it is! Play the game, but do not get wrapped up in this type of networking lifestyle. Instead, attend the events, shake lots of hands, be seen and make a quick, quiet exit. Avoid these types of environments as part of your normal routine; I guarantee that it is not worth losing your gift, dignity, professional focus, or internal peace.

Sometimes, opportunity waves itself in unhealthy environments—so always remember that opportunity comes in many forms.

View negative situations as a test of your character and know you are better than those situations. You do not have to compromise yourself or your gift to get ahead. It may take a little longer and you may have to work a little harder, but you will be able to sleep at night. You will not have made relationships that are destined to fail. Most importantly, you will not have compromised your dignity, integrity and character along the way.

Write down your thoughts about your personal and professional daily environments:

What is healthy about your current professional musical environment?

____

____

____

____

____

What and who should you keep around as you grow in your career?

____

____

____

____

____

____

What and who should not be in your presence and should be removed?

____

____

____

____

____

What is your plan to keep your environment abundant and in high vibration?

____

____

____

NEVER A SHORTAGE OF OPPORTUNITY

You Are A BORN Entrepreneur!

Become An Expert Within
The Business You Desire
To Work In. Study Your Craft And
Study The Business.

EMBRACE YOUR FULL NATURAL BEING

As women, we are constantly fighting against the perception of what we can and cannot do. The music industry is heavily male-dominated, making it even more important for a female artist like you to know the music business and have entrepreneurial wisdom. This is not just about general knowledge; it is essential to have a solid grasp of the various aspects and subsections of the music business. If you are a professional vocalist, you need to know enough about every part of the industry that touches your business, hired jobs and skill as a vocalist.

For example, when in the studio recording a song, you should understand the basic principles of the recording, mixing and mastering process—all the way down to the quality of the microphone being used. In addition, you should be able to speak intelligently at a high level about branding, marketing, project development and the strategy for your music projects, etc. Moreover, you should at least understand the basic concepts of the distribution process of your music (your investment).

The more information you know, the greater influence you hold as a woman. If you do not understand or know what is going on with your business and music projects, it will be easier for you to be taken advantage of. This is not just for women, men as well. Know your business, study, ask lots of questions and seek help when you are unsure about something!

Luckily, with the vastness of information the internet offers, you have an endless source of knowledge at your fingertips. A few hours of research each month can go a long way in establishing yourself as a knowledgeable professional in the industry.

Take time to understand your contracts, require contracts with people you work with and most importantly… **read your contracts**! Do not compromise on this to avoid someone's feelings or concerns about the working relationship. Business is business… it's not personal. It's just business!

Protect your investment and intellectual property; it is part of your legacy building process. Work with an attorney to review your contracts. Build relationships with entertainment attorneys before you need them; it would not hurt to have one on speed dial at all times!

Take the proper steps to own everything that has your name on it. Copyright all of your music before release and purchase your brand URLs NOW! Trademark your business, brand and stage name before you need to.

Also, reserve all social media handles for your brand, even if you do not plan to use them. Do not leave any brand social media handles open for others to use. It is your hard work, and you should get the credit and be the one making the money!

Some people and organizations make it their business mission to seek out great artists who have not taken the proper steps to trademark their brand or company name. Then, they trademark it behind the artist's back; the artist is left having to pay a licensing fee to use the name and brand they built. Do not let this happen to you! Never assume that people are not paying attention to you; whether you know it or not, they are!

Learn to manage your finances with confidence. As your finances grow, set checks and balances into place to ensure funds are managed properly. Review your financial accounts often. Sign all your checks, make sure you approve and sign off on everything connected to your brand name.

Take the time to build smooth work processes and operations, to ensure all elements of your business are covered. However, do not just take time to hone your skill—learn the business simultaneously. The more information you know, the better questions you will ask during your work experiences (and the more successful you will be throughout your journey).

In today's digital society, people can be whatever they choose to be. Anyone can start a business in 15 minutes with no experience. A person can be a photographer, producer or graphic designer (or at least say they are) with no credentials.

As a female artist, it is important to know your line of business. When you encounter individuals who say they can provide a service or product, you want to make sure they are true to the craft; can they provide the service and product you truly need? If you do not understand the basics involved with every component that touches your skill and business, you are more likely to waste unnecessary funds and valuable time.

For example, if you hire someone who is not skilled to meet your needs, you will end up with an inadequate product or service. As a result, you may have to start over, setting your project deadline back and depleting your budget.

Or worse, they could mess up all your hard work, brand or take advantage of your lack of knowledge. **KNOW YOUR BUSINESS!**

It is important to know exactly what you are getting yourself into as much as you possibly can. You can do this by studying and understanding the language, industries, systems, and processes that touch your skill, product, or service.

If an individual who does not have your best interest is aware that you are well-informed and not naïve, it helps to reduce the likelihood they will try and take advantage of the situation. They will be aware that you are knowledgeable and cannot be taken for a ride.

If an individual does not have your best interest in mind and you start asking the right questions, they will likely fade away and try to find someone else to take advantage of—because you are too much work for them. They know you are knowledgeable through your discussion as you are asking industry-related questions. They know that you will poke around and find the true answers to what is going on. Never underestimate the power of understanding the music business and sub-industries. **Knowledge is extremely powerful; use it as leverage and protection.**

Your art is only 20% of the pie; industry and business knowledge account for the rest—80%! If you truly want to be successful and full-heartedly, believe in your trusted gift…learn the music business or hire someone (you can trust) who does have the understanding. **All successful artists do this!**

Build a team and delegate; you have to invest (money) into yourself and your brand for it to grow. Your music business is no different than the popular local furniture store in your community. They invested in their business by hiring experts to build out their brand, storefront and advertisements, etc… if you are serious about your career, you will need to do the same. This is what separates successful artists from those who go nowhere. Successful artists embrace and build a business model that will produce results.

If you hire someone to handle the business side of your craft, you still need to know the business for checks and balances. At the end of the day, you are the CEO and should always be in control of your business, brand, finances and narrative.

Investing time to learn the music business does not take away from your talent or ability to create great music. In order to operate to your full potential and flourish, you have to embrace your full natural being. **You are a BORN entrepreneur and visionary**. Negotiation, calculation, influence and persuasion are natural skills that you have. Do not be afraid to exercise, develop and put your native entrepreneurial skills to work for you— **be unapologetic**!

Many of the world's greatest entrepreneurs have some type of a creative background. They took their gift of vision and married it with business to build unstoppable empires and you can do the same.

Write down how you truly feel about the business side of music:

Are you comfortable making business decisions for your brand? Be honest!

____

____

____

____

____

What is it about business that you are confident about?

____

____

____

____

What is it about the music business that scares you?

What music business skills should you strengthen or get help with?

____

____

List three potential mentors you can work with to develop stronger and more confident business skills. What date and time do you plan to reach out and schedule a time to meet with them?

____

____

____

____

____

____

Take Steps NOW To

Protect Your Privacy...

So You Do Not Have To Struggle

LATER To Protect Your Space, Money,

and Investments!

WHY SCRAMBLE LATER, DO THIS NOW

It is important to protect your privacy, including your physical address and any personal phone numbers. Take the time to establish a virtual business address and phone number. Your personal phone number, address and email should only be for close friends and family.

If you own property, work with an attorney to create a trust or entity that will keep your personal information associated with your properties and all investments private moving forward. Set up a virtual address at a local UPS store (or similar business provider) to forward all business mail and registration information. When you start to build your music business, you will be required to disclose an address for entities, such as your DBA,

LLC, copyrights, patents, trademarks, royalties, etc. The information you share with such entities is public information for the world; once it is out digitally, you cannot get it back.

Know that you will be successful. Move as though you are already where you want to be in your career. Do what successful people do. Take the proper steps to protect your privacy at the beginning of your musical journey, so you do not have to clean up a mess later... do it NOW!

Protecting your personal information does not sound like a big deal—until something goes wrong. Social media has changed the game! It is not just top celebrities who have crazy stalkers; people fall in love with the illusion of your "glamorous" life. It does not matter what level you are at in your career; you may encounter someone unstable or a person who wants something from you that is not work-related.

There are a couple of steps you can take to help protect your privacy. Create a Google phone number so you can control what time you receive phone calls and track who is calling. You can properly block numbers if needed without jeopardizing your personal phone number. You want to keep your personal phone number as confidential as possible. If the communication is work-related, give out your work phone number.

It is also smart to create a business email that only contains the information necessary for your work. Use the email on all online platforms, including social media accounts.

Also, be mindful about upcoming opportunities as well; protect your dream, career and vision! If you have a great opportunity coming up, keep it to yourself until it has been completed or 100% confirmed. Move in silence until the deal is closed! This process helps to protect the energy around your blessings and space. Wait until you know an opportunity is a 'done deal' before teasing the news on your social media platforms. Captivating and encouraging engagement online is important, but closing a long-awaited deal successfully is by far more important.

Write down all areas in your business that require the use of your personal information:

What elements do you currently have in place to protect your personal information as your brand and business grow?

____

____

____

____

____

What additional measures can you put into place now to protect your personal information moving forward?

____

____

____

____

WHY SCRAMBLE LATER, DO THIS NOW

____

____

You Are Trusted With

A Precious Light, Energy

And Gift. Do Not Casually Leave It

With Anyone.

A STAR IS A STAR

As a female recording artist, regardless of your age, do not go anywhere alone. It does not matter if you are just starting out or have been a professional recording artist for years. If you are going somewhere that requires you to be in a room with an individual who is not your husband, wife, sister, brother, father, mother, close friend, or trusted colleague, **do not go alone**.

If you are an artist starting out or do not have a large fan base compared to others, do not assume individuals are not paying keen attention to what you are doing. There are always people watching you, at all levels—never assume otherwise.

If you do not remember anything else in this book, please remember this: a star is a star, and a star is going to shine whether it's in earlier or later stages of its development.

Light attracts everything; the great, the good, the bad, and the ugly. You have to learn how to maneuver and decipher each type. People can see your light, and those who do not have your best interests in mind will try their chance with you—regardless of whether you are starting out or have built a name for yourself in the industry.

It is important to learn these lessons early in your career so as your career grows, you can keep yourself and your business safe. Know the types of individuals to keep around you and who to keep away.

Do not go anywhere alone, ever. Regardless of your age, physical strength, education or economic status. Even if you believe you can trust someone you just met, it is still important to operate cautiously and logically.

If you are in a situation where it is necessary to meet someone alone, make sure a trusted person is aware of your location and the time you are meeting. Collaboration is healthy and very important to your success, but ensure you are always collaborating in a safe manner. Do not assume you are automatically safe, no matter how 'trustworthy' you believe a person to be. Always bring someone with you when you can, and do not let your guard down. Choose public places when possible, especially when meeting or collaborating with someone for the first time.

It is essential to always keep your safety as a top priority, period.

It is unfortunate that this subject exists, but it is the reality we have always lived in. Now, however, women in music and other entertainment sectors are gaining the strength to talk about it more openly.

Write down your current in-person networking and collaborative practices:

What is your current safety plan when you meet new people?

____

____

____

____

____

Who will go with you or who will you contact when meeting new people? Is the person someone who will drop everything to come help or find you? If not, find someone who will!

____

____

____

____

____

____

Write down your top three emergency contacts; what information should you provide them NOW to ensure you are located quickly if needed?

____

____

____

____

____

____

A Star Is A Star And
People Can See It $$$$$,
Even If You Cannot!

UGLY TRUTH...
THE MALE GROUPIE

Yes, there is such a thing as a male groupie, and ladies, take note; you do not have to be a megastar to have groupies! I never thought about this until I started singing with a band alongside our male lead singer. I would watch how the female groupies would show up front row whenever our band was performing. They were constantly falling head over heels for our Jamaican dreadlock-wearing lead vocalist. That experience helped me realize you do not have to be a mega superstar to have groupies.

It is true; Joe Blow down the street with the rock band or Michael Walker around the block with the rap group has groupies. When you understand the power of your gift, you will realize you do not have to be performing in a sold-out venue to hold a level of presence and star power. These qualities are evident whether you are known only in your local community or traveling worldwide and appearing on TV screens.

As I started to notice the males in our band receiving groupie attention, I also noticed there were male fans who were latching onto me and another female counterpart in the band. It took me by surprise—it was one of the weirdest things I had ever felt or encountered. I thought, 'hey, I'm not a superstar, I'm just Latoya who sings in the local band. So why are these men head over for me? I am someone they do not know, yet they are asking for dates and the opportunity to call me personally.

As I branched out and started working more aggressively as an independent artist, I noticed a shift; I noticed the male groupies were still around, but their tactics were very different; they were more subtle and quiet, such as standing in the back of the room, and approaching me after a show offering free services or connections. They were always working to find a way to gain my personal information or become connected to me on a personal level. I learned the workings of the male groupie very quickly.

It is not uncommon for women who work as recording artists or performers to fall for the basic male groupie.

The male groupie is very different from the female groupie, so let me break it down for you: the male groupie often wants to quickly get into your personal life. They want to know your phone number, where you live, possibly date you—things of that nature. They may even try to influence or control your career if they get close enough to you. This is something to be mindful of, especially as a woman. It is hard to be completely sure of the intentions they may have. You can be someone who sings with the local band in the community and still have male groupies who become obsessed (in some cases become stalkers). I am not trying to scare you; I am simply sharing a possible reality with you.

Do not promise anything to a fan that may potentially place you in an unsafe situation. In addition, never share personal information with a fan. If someone wants to get in contact with you, refer them to your manager, give them a business card or share a Google phone number with them. Alternatively, you could take their information and follow up on your terms. This gives you time to ensure the information provided is accurate and legitimate.

Male groupies are not always as obvious as female groupies. For most of us, we know how the stereotypical female groupie acts; she is often screaming at the top of her lungs at the front of the stage. She may be grabbing for the artist or sitting in the back of a venue, giggling, pointing, flirting and admiring the talent on the stage. We have all seen this stereotype in some form, if not in real life, on TV, or in movies. However, the male groupie is much more strategic with his target.

If you are not in tune with the male groupie, they can become wolves and vultures in your life. Any human, regardless of gender, can bring toxicity to your life if you are not mindful. For the moment, however, we are focused on the male groupie. If the male groupie is able to get past a certain barrier or boundary within your circle, he can wreak havoc—especially if his intentions are not healthy.

Often, the male groupie is someone who is interested in you on a physical level and head over heels with the illusion of your brand and/or persona. These are people who, more often than not, know little about your true personal life or the requirements and demands of your growing music career. If they did know more, they probably would not be so fascinated. The music business is not easy!

As you move forward in your musical career as a woman and entrepreneur, take this situation for what it is and nothing more. Watch out for the male groupie!

Write down how you feel about the male groupie:

Is this something you have thought about and can identify around you?

____

____

____

____

____

____

How do you plan to manage the male groupie as your career grows?

____

____

____

____

Love Has Nothing To Do With It... Bullet-proof Your Music Career And Business!

CLOSE THE DEAL FIRST!

It is important you understand how male-dominated the music industry is. Men are physical and like to admire beauty, so you are likely being sized up the moment you walk in the door. When you are working in new environments, be very clear through your actions, vocal tone and demeanor that you are there to work—not to be someone's boy toy. Creating music does not require a physically intimate relationship with the people you work with. You find love when you find love, but it is important to always look at the situation for what it is. Everyone is present to do a job, not to start a physical relationship that is more than likely going to distract or deter you from your initial goals.

CLOSE THE DEAL FIRST!

If you decide to start a consensual physical relationship with someone you work with, make sure it compliments your professional growth. Make sure there are career-launching benefits in it for you!

Personally, I have seen scenarios where women got involved with someone they worked with and it jeopardized the growth of their music career. You have to weigh what is most important for you.

I would recommend getting the job done first! Ensure your projects are completed and the record deal is signed before entering into a physical relationship with someone who could possibly end all of the hard work and investments you have put in. This does not mean you cannot have both. You can; just make sure you are using your head first, then your heart when it comes to business... the music business!

The more you know about the business, the quicker you can make judgment on how to handle each situation. Ask yourself questions like, 'is this real love or another distraction? Does this person sincerely care about my personal and career growth?' Ask objective questions. Clear thinking is power.

If you are dating the fan, aka the male groupie, know that they will not be receptive to other people being close to you, male or female. They will not be fond of people who are in your circle or others who admire you. This is because they do not understand the nature and environment of your work and often cannot handle what it requires.

Without being aware, you may end up dating a male groupie or someone who is obsessed with you. These individuals can become abusive, isolate you or grow to control you and your gift. Again, this is not to scare you, but a reminder to be vigilant of this type of thing happening.

It does not matter if you are singing at the local church or on a huge stage across the world; performers are admired by many people and it can be intimidating to someone who is insecure and wants to control your environment.

CLOSE THE DEAL FIRST!

Be aware of wolves and vultures. Sometimes they will show up, not as groupies, but in other ways as well. If you listen and trust your instinct and discernment, these internal guides will cover you on many different levels.

This is why spirituality and your relationship with the Lord are important. When you encounter a person or situation that you sense to be unhealthy, connect spiritually and trust (inner voice) to guide and maneuver you out. This is crucial if you need to back away from an agreement, arrangement, commitment, relationship, or situation that does not sit well with your inner being (your guide). Learn to trust yourself without question or regret. What does not work out for you, works out for you!

Write down your thoughts about dating in music, be honest with yourself:

Do you find yourself dating people you work with often? How do you plan to bullet-proof your growing career in the process?

____

____

____

____

____

How do you plan to close deals first so that you can have the career and love in a close work environment?

____

____

____

____

73

Define your limitations and boundaries when it comes to love in the workplace?

Heal Your Trauma...

Leave No Fuel For Those

Who Come To Steal, Kill and Destroy

Your Energy & Light.

WOLVES, VULTURES & NARCISSISTS

If you are planning to have a music career, it is wise to study the intricate aspects associated with various personality traits and disorders. It may sound crazy, but this knowledge will come in handy big time!

It is common to see narcissistic personalities and more aggressive forms of personality disorders among various people within the music industry. I am not a psychologist or psychiatrist (psychotherapist), so I do not know why this is, but my assumption is that it is due to the music and entertainment industry being so glorified. Certain types of personalities seek to be seen and worshiped… and in the music community, there is the opportunity for just that (as well as a lot of power).

These personalities are not only present in the music but also in other types of business industries. Unfortunately, they are often seen at high-level positions within organizations and companies. They all have the same motivations—seeking the power of control and validation. I bring this point up because, once again, the music industry is heavily male-dominated. Even though women can carry these types of personality traits, they are more dominant within the male population of this industry.

Understanding these personality types will help you avoid situations that may not be healthy for you. When you are able to understand the patterns, how these particular personalities operate and attempt to 'groom' their potential victims, you are less likely to fall prey to their toxic mission.

These personalities seek to destroy; they destroy everything they encounter and everyone in their path. When you see them coming, stay calm, guide the encounter and exit—quickly, peacefully and unharmed.

These types of personalities will destroy without remorse.

Hear me very clearly; **you cannot manage or maintain a healthy relationship with these types of personalities.** They do not respect boundaries nor have limits to what they will do to get what they want.

Study and understand their commonality so you can foresee their possible movements as early as possible.

The more you learn about these traits, the less intimidating they are, and the better chance you have of staying one step ahead. These people only care about themselves and no one else. They only want something specific from you—your energy—which serves as a supply source for them (like a vampire).

They will disregard you and leave you to the wayside without thinking twice once they have sucked you dry. These people have very dark spirits; they are sent to dim your light and destroy your gift.

Live your life with your light shining bright. Do not let anyone or anytime stand in the way of your greatness and happiness.

You will see these personality trails at all levels, in management, co-workers, family members and within possible love interests.

The great thing is more people are openly talking about narcissism or personality disorders, which helps to build knowledge and awareness.

If you are a person who is a compassionate giver by nature, you are more likely to be a target for narcissists. On the other hand, if you are an empath or have codependency issues, you are wearing a bullseye on your forehead... sorry to break it to you!

They will see a gold mine within you because you have a giving heart and are empathetic towards others. You are the perfect target for them because they can take, and they know you will give. They will take more and more, and you will continue to give because it is in your nature—draining you until you have nothing left to give.

Learn to identify these vampires right away, so you can move on as quickly as you can!

Remember: you always hold your power. Do not let these personalities convince you of anything you know in your heart to be untrue. They know you hold a powerful light and want it for themselves, but you get to decide whether or not to give it to them. Never give your purpose-filled mighty powerful light (your gift) to anyone, but if you feel as though you already have, know that it is never too late to take it back.

Research these personalities. There are many books and quick resources available for you to analyze these types of personality traits. In addition, there are countless videos on YouTube where many experts share an abundance of knowledge regarding this topic. There are even videos available discussing how prevalent these types of individuals are in the music and entertainment space and how to identify them.

Do not let anyone take away your dream, slow down your dream, or distract you from your dream because of their selfish, destructive actions. Again, hold on to your power, and protect your power (your light, your energy source).

Do not let anyone drain or suck the life out of you. These people will work and strive to drain every bit of beauty from your heart, mind, body and soul. As mentioned before, if you find yourself in a situation where you feel like this is happening, remember that it is never too late to get out.

Write down your thoughts about narcissism and personality disorders:

Do you see people around you with narcissistic traits? Are they in your personal or work life?

____

____

____

____

____

What checks and balances can you put into place to make sure they do not suck the life out of you... seriously!?!?

____

____

____

____

____

____

How will you minimize or eliminate these types of
personalities from your life?

____

____

____

____

____

If you have codependency issues, what professional help will you seek to find out why? What techniques will you use moving forward to end codependency or at least manage it within yourself?

____

____

____

____

____

____

Like You First, Love You First And

Draw Your Line...

The Right People Will Like

And Love You Back!

SAVVY, SMART, SEXY NON-NEGOTIABLES

You cannot control what others do. What you can control is holding yourself to a healthy standard and expectation—which influences how others positively treat you.

People should treat you with respect at all times regardless of the situation. Unfortunately, society is not set up that way. Take what you know and make it work for you—game it before it games you!

One of the most valuable things you can do for yourself is to know your self-worth, have standards and set boundaries. Never compromise or negotiate in this area. These are things that will help keep you safe and decrease the number of people in your circle who do not have your best interest at heart. When you know your worth, you will not tolerate anything that is not reflective of your standards. Set clear boundaries and always stick to them—even if it costs you an opportunity or a working relationship. Stick to your boundaries! Learn to strategically manage relationships above and below you, including your boss.

You do not want to be a part of anything that does not sit well with you, only to regret it later. A lot of women find themselves in situations they are not proud of later on in life. This is because they either did not know their self-worth or were not willing to reinforce solid boundaries. Much of this is rooted in the social conditioning of girls and women, to be seen, not heard and to be agreeable at all times—regardless of what is happening to them. As a result, women often compromise in areas they are not comfortable with, possibly out of fear, intimidation, desire to be loved, or pressure to be accepted.

If you are not comfortable with something, do not do it! If you are not at peace with what is asked of you, speak up for yourself. If you are not comfortable, reiterate your boundaries. Opportunity always comes around. Do not compromise your standards or boundaries for an opportunity. Always question any opportunity that requires you to compromise your boundaries. Do not let anyone persuade you to do something you are uncomfortable with; your uneasy feeling is valid. Stand up for yourself. Your safety and health are a priority. **Your NO is a non-negotiable**. Define your line!

You will make some people mad along the way, be okay with it! They may be mad, but they will respect you. **There is nothing more savvy, smart and sexy than your non-negotiable NO!**

Remember, anything that comes from a place of calling, purpose and full alignment will not require you to do things that are harmful to yourself in order to receive elevation in your life.

Write down your thoughts about self-worth:

How do you feel about your personal self-worth, self-esteem and confidence?

____

____

____

____

____

Are you comfortable establishing clear boundaries personally and professionally? If so, what are your non-negotiables?

____

____

____

____

____

____

What can you do to strengthen your confidence and maintain healthy boundaries in your life as you move forward in your career?

____

____

____

____

____

Everything Has A Price;

It May Not Be Money...

It Could Be More Expensive.

MORE VALUABLE THAN MONEY

Have you heard the saying *'nothing in life is free'*? This is especially true in the music business. Ask questions if anyone offers you something for free. There are people who do great things out of the kindness of their hearts, so you should not be wary of everyone. What you should do instead is ask direct questions related to each unique situation. Always document all transactions, even if someone is offering you something for free. Make sure you have some sort of documentation referencing the final communication of that free transaction. You want to make sure you do not owe anyone money or any services and that nothing can be used against you at a later time.

A great practice to incorporate is to **always pay something**, even if it is just a few dollars for the "FREE" service. This will communicate a clear *paid-for services* trail.

It is unfortunate that you have to be conscious of this and work to make sure you are protected. As I mentioned before, you are working in a male-dominated industry, and you are a woman. You need to know that there are people who will try to take advantage of you simply for being a woman. This is even more likely if you do not know the business well. I highly recommend you learn as much as you can about general business practices and the music business itself, so you can fully understand the conversations you will have with people day to day (and what it may cost you).

Your internal peace, physical safety, soul and life mission is more valuable than any dollar amount. No amount of money can fix, repair or substitute what is priceless, YOU.

Write down your thoughts about taking free services or products during your music career journey:

How do you plan to manage bartering in your growing career?

____

____

____

____

____

What checks and balances will you use to manage these types of situations in your career?

____

____

____

____

Play Life Full Out...

Get Comfortable Going Against The Grain!

LEAD OR GO HOME

Leadership and confidence will take you far within the music business. As a woman, it is critical you master the skills of leadership and confidence within your every daily work decisions. In this industry, you must grow thick skin, a strong backbone and the ability to speak up for yourself. Be decisive and strong enough not to compromise on what you know is right for what you need in order to cultivate your career. You have to be able to carry your own and be unapologetic about it. Yet, still hold dear and use your femininity, work every angle to your advantage. Your feminine energy and essence are your ultimate leverage and power.

There is an art to exercising the power of NO while avoiding a negative impact on your work relationships (learn this talent). You do not want to burn bridges, but you do want to stand your ground and establish clear boundaries. Be sure to speak clearly and with confidence. There is no room for meek behavior or personality in the music industry. Be bold, be fearless! People want to work with individuals who are confident and organized. Be self-assured in what you are doing and have a solid sense of direction. If you are not sure, ask for help from an expert. Be in charge of your business in every aspect.

Do not be afraid to fire and hire the right people. Do not be timid to ask for what you want in a clear and direct manner.

Remember, there is no friendship in business—there are only business relationships. Understand this very clearly; it will help remove the personal sensitivity in your work relationships. Focus on the health of your business and providing great service to your customers, fans and work partnerships.

Culturally, confident women in leadership roles can still be hard to digest for some. However, in order to have a successful music business, you must be gutsy and courageous—make epic moves!

Develop a wide variety of skills such as leadership, networking, negotiation, and communication, that will teach you how to stand firm while you build. If you are not confident negotiating on your own behalf, providing instruction and leading the way for your team and fans, the music business is not the place for you.

Get cozy and comfortable in your own skin; work on developing this first—know who you are. If you are not sure what that looks like for you, take time to study, dig deeper within yourself, and put professional recommendations into play toward owning what makes you a superpower.

If you are serious about your music career, you must first master leadership and confidence, or go home!

Write down your thoughts on your current leadership practices and types:

What steps will you take to strengthen your leadership skills?

____

____

____

____

____

What practices do you plan to put into place to learn more about yourself—become more comfortable with who you are?

____

____

____

____

____

____

What are some steps you can take to build your confidence?

____

____

____

____

____

FINAL WORDS

You have a right to be protected. Your gift and what it produces have a right to be protected. You cannot control the actions of others. However, you have a right to take steps and measures to protect yourself and your trusted gift. Again, knowledge is power!

Take what you have learned from this book today, apply and revisit it throughout your career. Use the content in this book to remind yourself why it is so important to stay protected—you have valuable work to do with your trusted gift!

Apply these *simple methods* for *smarter decisions*. Share this book with other women; look out for each other! Help other women and young girls in the business stay protected and move like the boss they were born to be.

Let this book serve as the beginning of a meaningful conversation within your music community. Work together and share how we can continue to be safe as women, yet still achieve our music career goals.

May God continue to bless you in your endeavors and journey. Focus on making God the center of your musical mission, and always use your gift for good. Do not be persuaded by money, fame, social pressure, or attention and lose sight of your purpose-filled intentions. Maintain your standards, stand your ground and move forward with integrity.

If you ever feel uneasy about a decision you are on the verge of making, or an opportunity that sits in front of you, take a step back. Anytime you are unsettled about something, there is a reason for it; re-evaluate, then take action! It is your instinct and discernment bringing something forward for you to be vigilant about. **Do not be afraid to listen to your womanly instinct; it is a**

gift God has given you... and even more, it is a blessing.

Do not question yourself—always go with what you know is right.

Here at Music Meets The Boardroom, we are dedicated to your success. We want to see you win in every area of your growing music business.

Let us know how we can help you move forward powerfully and purposefully in the music industry. Do not hesitate to contact us; we want to hear from you!

You got this SuperStar! :-)

ABOUT THE AUTHOR

LATOYA COOPER, also known as "The Songstress", is the founder of **MUSIC MEETS THE BOARDROOM**, the *#1 Platform For Top A-List Indie Artist Entrepreneurs*. Latoya is a successful self-sustained businesswoman sought after by music industry channels for her expertise and fresh direct approach.

Latoya has spent the past decade in the project management space and holds a Master's of Business Administration.

Latoya is a born VISIONARY, an accomplished Recording and Touring Artist, Entrepreneuress and has been featured on Essence.com as "The Artist To Watch"!

Latoya uses her extensive know-how to help Indie Artists shift their business model from surviving to thriving by leading with their Superpower, nurturing their entrepreneurial traits, and building a clear plan of action toward achieving their BIGGEST CAREER GOALS!

Learn more about Latoya Cooper and her services at: **www.LatoyaCooper.com**.

Connect with Latoya Cooper on: TikTok, Instagram, LinkedIn, Youtube, Facebook and Twitter.

JOIN THE MUSIC MEETS THE BOARDROOM MOVEMENT

VISION: A Community Of 1,000 Thriving A-list Indie Artist Entrepreneurs Who Find Purpose, Self-empowerment And Strategy To Execute God's Plan For Their Gift.

MISSION: We Help A-List Indie Artist Entrepreneurs Find Their Superpower and Build A Powerful Plan For Action.

Visit MusicMeetsTheBoardroom.com For More Information About Our Services!

Register For The Annual Indie Artist Power Conference: www.musicmeetstheboardroom.com/schedule/indie-artist-power-conference